The Pursuit of Love and Happiness

CHAPTER

To Bahedile Pheko, Ketlareng Pheko and Moroke Pheko

It is all in your head, make your mind the best place to be. Let it be where your flowers grow, where you find your glow. Water it and appreciate everything that emerges. Let your emotions flow.

1. Unspoken words

Be sure the company you keep is the one that aims to do the same; to keep and cherish you

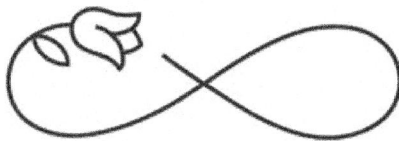

-we choose who we become by choosing who stays in our lives

Sweet Creature

The moon dances over your good side

Your tongue tells stories that never have been told

Your heart beats to the stream of the riverside

And makes us the promise of happiness till we're old

The sun kisses your innocent face

And the trees smell like your kindness

The ocean moves only at your pace

And brings us all into your loveliness

M MOKGOTHU

Not your fairy-tale song

Or a friend to do you wrong.

Not your everyday cup of tea

She's everything you do not usually see.

On her artery I have never crossed

Yet not a road I would ever get lost.

Of powerful delight, the glory of her might

Of striking words, it is the way she shines so bright.

Beautiful and devoted you have been

Now Pen has made you her queen.

And so that you sit at the throne

You are more fearless of the unknown.

She carries her heart as a canvas

And the Almighty as her compass.

Off all sorts of things, the canvas is painted each day

She just laughs and journeys with it all the way.

TUNES OF THE SILVER TRUMPET

I hear the soothing tunes that make my dear.

I hold it to my heart when I am in disarray

I could feel the coldness of a well-worked art piece

One that awaited the right artist.

The silver trumpet is not like any other trumpet.

It is a friend to a lonely boy

A companion when all friends have gone.

I then remember the tone of the old Da Vinci

"Art is never finished, only abandoned"

That is when the melody of a heartfelt song begins.

A melody that was quickly abandoned when I heard the sound of my friends' footsteps

Pitter-patter! Pit-a-pat!

I play it under the rising stars of the night.

Seeing as my closest star has gone,

Gone not for long as I remember it always returns.

And I could see my friends yet again.

But for now I will only play the melody.

With my fingers on the silver valves.

With my mouthpiece on my crack-ed lips.'

With the tune perfectly intertwined,

With the memory of a well-spent day.

SWEETFACE

I know that you are my best,

Pumping my heart faster than the rest.

Breaking the silence of my emotions,

Igniting the passion of love.

And today I got to see the better of you,

If not the best of you.

How can one be so beautiful?

How can nature make so perfect a sculpture?

I am not one to answer these questions or to ask them.

All I need is to look at you, really look at you.

Your eyes are a healing.

Your mouth a different feeling.

I get lost in your reverie

Every second thinking of you.

Maya Rakoteli

With your binaural hearing you heard even the silent cries

With tendered heart, your love came as no surprise

You do not have the fairest vision

But you see me through angel eyes

Your faith in me is perhaps the greatest thing

And your words of wisdom are the strongest shield

They led me from the temperament of comfort

To an uncharted river of light waters

Water that I drank to grow my youthful mind

Like the owl, they may perceive as the harbinger of death

Yet you have brought life to me

You have shown me the real life to be led

You are a goddess of wisdom and preciousness

You are a fine art. A living reminder,

That there is still some kindness left in this void

LUNA

Diamond of the sky

In the darkness where you shine

Keeper of kindness, ruler of the tides

You smile without shyness, and all anger subsides.

You have been put above us,

Yet you are the humblest amongst us.

You are a ruler of no country,

But we all fall in your bounty.

Luna, sis pulchrior quam ego sum

I am jealous, perfect cannot be this perfect.

You are my best, my friend, my enemy and my lover.

Let us not tell our truth too late.

And fall for Solis and her bait.

The Last One

I wish this to be more than a poem but a letter

I wish my parting with you would be by death

It would bring the best romance our love never had

You were right for me for some time

The kisses we stole from each other brought

the mystery in our romance that I had longed for

The gift of comfort you gave to me was enough for some time

And I hope my gifts to you did the same.

But it wasn't until it was too late that I realised it wasn't love

You were only an experience in a very long time

that my mind desired but which my soul rejected

Now we part. You may not have died for me,

but at some point that is what I would've done for you.

Unspoken words

Actions so little do as much

But few words light a fire in the heart

There is a sense of homeliness in love

Shown through the mere arrangement of letters

There is comfort in appreciation

That endears us the afflicted the same way it endears the
speaker

Words like these are protection and a silver lining

Words like these bring life to our beloved

So why then are they only said at funerals?

Why are they uttered at the coming of death?

These words fall onto deaf ears

They lose meaning if they are heard by enemies

They lose meaning, they leave us all disconsolate

But all rested is the supposed receiver,

Who wishes they were said while she was still alive.

11. The Power of Love

The bravest thing you will ever do is to learn how to love

- the things we bleed of and the things we bleed for

LOOK

Look into her eyes like maybe

She is magic

Look into her eyes like you

Would look at the rivers.

Look at her like you can see

Your true self in the story she tells.

Look at her like maybe your life

Would fade away if you turned away.

Your sentiments are in all

She has to offer.

A repertoire of emotions,

A dance of dragons.

Fire burns inside her eyes

A passion of love.

ELECTRIC LOVE

You are like lightning in the water

You torture me like I don't even matter

You make me feel like a beggar

Yet I still fall for you better

There is no need to take it slow

Your love is toxic, we are already on death row

When you die, I'll still feel the current

It takes a toll on me and leaves me just,

It is the necessary evil I burn for.

Your electric love, Voltage higher than my rage.

Burning the sun and annihilating the moon.

Bringing the darkness to the light and leaving the ocean dry.

You take my breath away and I am left to gape for the toxins
you feed me.

You destroy me but I love it.

In some way, the way you do it makes it feel homely

Long as I am loved by you and this love is enough.

Electric Love.

I will never fall in love till I find a copy of your heart,

You are that mortal-eternal kind of love.

All around me

Wear my heart and I'll wear yours,

I will take the things in your inner cores.

If it be of a greater cause.

Then my dearest, you dare not to pause

You are my ocean and my dream

I drown in you with lucid pleasure.

You are my heart and my moon,

You are my life and my greatest treasure.

Let us watch everything amidst

Embrace me my love, let the wind blow

Let them go west and we'll go east

Our compass is greater, the greatest roads it will show.

Love, for what it is

I am no longer the strayed dog

I am no more a slave to fear

I am no longer a reckless driver

I am a changed and reformed addict.

Things have changed, you need to understand

I need you to know that I'm the person that you have always
wished for me to be

I am the person you once fell in love with but was too blinded
by the swarm of bees to see your honest affection

I am a changed man, changed to my former self.

And I am feeling that to tell you this is a truth I have always
wanted you to know

I want you to know that I love you and I am sorry for always
waiting till tomorrow

Tomorrow when things changed and the I could tell myself
that now the time is right

Yet my cowardly self would not let me release what is inside of
my eyes

I love you more than I could say

I may not have always shown it

I may have always put you in second place

At that time I told myself I did not love you

But the truth is it was always love,

It was love for what I knew love to be.

Ocean eyes

Those brown eyes,

So perfect like a twilight.

So flawless and gazing in the night,

I can't help but fall in the tide.

When I look at you I tend to rewind.

Because I can't help but fall in your ocean eyes.

All of you is too perfect, all too right.

Your eyes trapped me and I cannot escape.

I tried ruining you, I tried to ruin your eyes,

But I realised I too would be blind.

Because I cannot see in a world without you

I cannot be myself when I am not around you.

Your beauty exposes the weakness of my heart

Because my love for you is infinite, indefinite.

It's not waiting for you to be complete,

It does not want you to compete.

You are perfect the way you are

That is the beauty of your charm.

And if you have imperfections,

They were probably drowned by your ocean eyes.

I love you because you are who you are,

And you own up to what you are.

I love you because in you I can drown and still feel alive.

Lost love

There are an infinite number of days

When I listened to the song in your eyes

When the innocence in your unchartered face

Inveigled me more than words dare to mesmerise

I remember the dream of you as on my bed I lay

It lasted long enough to be a thousand years

In the period I had been so much in disarray

Because I always woke up with dry salty tears

But now we are scattered around the place

Our journey was suddenly cut short

I was besotted, only moving at your pace

Did not realise that for me, it was a lot

What's left is the mockery of our misfortune

A stagnant wheel, unturned through day and dawn

Our story, of stolen glimpses and exhaustion

Now my love has lost the will to carry on.

Another Love

I would give my life for one more night

If a minute with you would last forever

Your darkness builds the corners of my heart

Time is all I have now in this endeavour

The fruits of your trees are sweet like sin

You bring out the thorns in my rose

My heart takes things so forbidden

This was never the life I chose

Your fragrance of subtle cruelty melts my soul

Takes away all things I've known to own

Ever so charming is your guilty face

That I forget your faults and rest my case

Just Someone

Someone to kiss, someone to miss

Someone to take your breathe

Someone to pour life into you

Just someone to be there

I promise to bring you bliss

More than there is on this earth

To be your sunshine in the blue

To be always in your special care

Glory to my Lover

I want to rest in your kisses

I want only to dream of you

Holding your hand on magic bridges

One that holds our love over and under the blue

When you say my name in your sweet voice

Let the winds blow to caress your love in me

I want the sun through the trees to rejoice

And you like the earth to bring me to my knees

I want your light to bend over like the sunflower

Your love that is deeper than the rain

To be there when I forfeit my power

Only you can keep me out of this chain

Crosses

Is it perhaps the way you look at me?

That taught mine eyes to see

Is it the way you remember me?

That gives my mind its memory

Is it the way you love me?

That taught my heart its beat

The way you touch me

That my fingers would cross with yours

Perhaps it is the way you look at me

That taught my eyes true beauty

The way you remember me

That gave my mind its greatest treasure

The way in which you love me

That I always cross my heart

Your frail and unpredictable gestures

That I hope to die in your arms

The Power of your love

There is a song in the way you look at me

A form of nostalgia in the way you speak

There are things that only you can do

To my fragile body which longs for your mysterious touch

Your love is demanding, and I give my all

Giving you my all just so I could feel

Even the sun does not have this surge over me

It lights me now, but you burn my world forever

Loving you is like holding the thorns of a rose

There is pain in the love you give me

You are an immaculate dream of wonder

Perfectly immersed in the ocean of mystery

Far and near, you take my breath

To the peak of an enchanted mountain

At the top of it all. Where life meets death

III. GOLDEN

Sometimes you have to find time to discover yourself, learn who you truly are. To sit at the table with every part of yourself. All the horrors, insecurities, fears, our happy and lonely selves. To talk and to cry, to laugh, so that in the end we make peace with who we are.

-the bitter times that give life

SPEAK!

The loud bells are loud no longer,

The yelling of the ton is now softer.

The readers have lost interest,

They care less about you than they do the rest.

So why then are you not free?

Why do you feel that you still ought to be somehow in the right depth of the ocean?

You are screaming for peace, but we cannot hear you.

You are gasping for breath, but we cannot hold you, touch you.

Why?

Why?

Why do you let yourself in the encumbrances of the past?

We will care for you no longer! Than to let ourselves suffer again.

Speak!

For if you do you will be content.

Do not end the life that keeps on giving

Do not return this gift, it would be rude

Be the hero of oneself and subdue sadness...

It holds your life at this moment, you are screwed.

Your silence is as loud as hail.

Killing you inside, the outside is pale.

Give me a page to rid of this rage,

Give me a sword, so I can do far better than words.

Give me your heart, maybe I can restart.

ELATION

Take off the band aid

Annihilate the man's curse

Turn off the sadness

And on is the happiness

We are the warriors of peace

We are the advocates of joy

We are sail men for your troubles

Let them sail away through with the stream

Let the sun burn the pains and rotten habits

And let the blossoming sunflower be a symbol of a new kind of
feeling... one you have awaited at the shore of emotions

Feel the elation

Be glad you were there, waiting all this time

It does not last for long

But you have remained strong

God knows why you held on.

HOW IS TIME TRAVEL POSSIBLE?

We are altered by your mere existence

We are steered by your mere presence.

You lose and treasure all of my memories.

And I relive all of my joys and sorrows.

Your image is of grotesque stature,

Leaving us to our wretched nature.

If only I could rewind and refill the dying well.

To make me whole and complete with will.

The bittersweet dreams I have,

I envy them to be my renaissance.

The nightmares of my worst terrors,

The horrors of my worst nightmares.

Take me back, take me hither.

Take me somewhere, take me far away.

Take me to see my soul in the mirror.

For my life only I can portray.

TO THE MIRROR OF MY SOUL

I have sinned and I have perforated you

I have made a bargain I could not uphold

I have made promises to this world that have altered your
beauty

There is no purity in me, no form of innocence

As cold as ice, as wild as fire.

Now I burn for the past, I burn for the renaissance I see only
in my dreams

How horrible it is that this is the day the birds lose their wings

The sun loses its shine

Like all of these you lose the innocence you once held

Losing it to the world to which you give your all

The world from which you seek true elation.

Yet be blessed in this wonder of life.

Be blessed in the madness of this world

And that you still revive and seek the beauty in all of it

They do not know what lies beneath the surface

What lies beneath the pity things that people say feed their
souls these days

There is no use to dwell in all this horror

The mystery lies in why we hold on

Even when there is nothing to hold onto

Let us be happy, let us be glad.

Let us celebrate the chaos we see as the ladder to the peak of
our lives

The eyes to which we shall see true beauty

The mirror of my soul, I cannot make you pure

I can only make you enjoy the littlest of life that you have left.

Dream of a broken boy

Oh! My first love, first time.

In my dreams there are infinite scenes

Where I take you so to be my bride

Where we are so elated on the greens

With the sun hitting so lightly

That it forgets to wake me up

I take you by my arms so tightly

Then with your love you fill my cup

Oh dear! I with fault arise from this dream

My senses so exhausted from this exercise

I had only a glimpse of this life, at fifteen

I never had the thought it would be my demise

From then I fell for you out of pity

In the end it's ended pleasure I feel guilty

Golden

There are parts of me, perfectly hidden

Some I do not know if they still exist

They stay forever in my thoughts, handwritten

So deep you could not catch them if you fished

They make the eternal verities of my heart

They coordinate the pieces of me you see today

So forgive me if I feel you've caught me off guard

But there is a lot to me that I cannot say

I do not want you to understand or try

They are amorphous, imperfect and have amazing glow

They are the reason of why sometimes I cry

Yet they leave me pure on the outside like snow

They are hidden beautifully in my scars and in pen

I will show you when you never have to see me again

IV. BY THE WATER

To all the people who loved me, to the ones who built me a future they thought I deserve. To the friends and family who stand beside me at all times

-thoughts of a better life

Fading Stars

We are so high and far behind

We are the plague and the bright light

Reminding them of what they once felt

Giving them the pieces of what is left

You move me with your flounce reaction

You shoot above with earnest passion

Your fiery eyes gives me compassion

An uncommon kind of love; but our own fashion

Our love may have ended

I am sorry for where I ever offended

I crossed dangerous roads unintended

Until such time too late to have mended

MOTHERLAND

Madiba! Your departure was a deep sorrow.

We are lost and we cannot see.

Oh! If only there was time we could borrow.

Then we could exist the way we ought to be.

Mzansi is fettered, she is a ruin, she is bitter and sour.

We have lost Ubuntu; lost humility and we have lost hope.

Oh! Implore heaven to return you, we need you at this hour.

To guide her, she is confused, now we cannot cope.

We still remember you were here like a phoenix.

To leave a legacy of freedom, power and virtue.

For us to take care of the tranquil land and all its scenic.

You are truly a moving monument, not only in your statue.

Tata Madiba! We will live your legacy.

To preserve your message, to honour your excellency.

GODSPEED

The dauntless solicitude that shielded me.

Your fearless operation that wielded me.

I am a sharpened sword of bravery.

When the marching band entered our premises.

When the women lit their candles and made empty promises.

That is when I wished that perhaps I had doves,

That I had 21 guns and men to shoot in black gloves.

It was a quiet day; the birds sang no longer.

It was a sad day, but my heart was beating stronger.

You were my love, my life, my everything.

You were my strength and my preacher.

You taught me how to stand firm.

You gave me hope and was my healer.

You are still, the well from which I drink my water.

But it is time I bid you farewell.

The sky has been ready to receive you,

But I held on, hoping to always have a part of you.

But now I am ready to let go.

Godspeed sister. Godspeed mother.

Only angel

Under the deformity of my love she's still here

Singing sweet songs of peace in the brink

Of war, of the selfishness of this vacuum

For which I so give my only existence.

She guides my foolish thoughts with special care

She takes my hand gently, so I do not sink

Not only do I always go away so soon

I also miss the delight of her amazing presence.

She reminds me every day how valuable she is!

My sweet, my angel in borrowed robes

It is her faith that strengthens my broken heart

She carries me under white wings that lift me up.

She puts herself in danger,

She gives her love tirelessly.

She is my guardian, my Angel.

For her I would give my life endlessly.

Mockingbird

She is as short as you'd like,

But as loud as the mockingbird.

This young and gentle maid,

With kindness that gives me sight.

She is as she has always been

Even when things were not as they were

So fearless, she is something I have not seen

Her nimbus spirit is clean and ever so fair

Of course our journey together has ended,

She was heartbroken when we had turmoil.

I with broken heart came back and mended,

Took out our precious treasure from the soil.

You have been true and loyal.

You have been fair and royal.

You are all I had hoped for,

Even I couldn't ask for more.

By the water

The water hits at our feet as we sit.

The ocean takes with my tears as it waves goodbye

It takes my breathe away to an endless pit

Where all burdens on my shoulders will now reside.

But the ocean, that big ocean, is not the real healer

But much more the friend who is always there

The friend who carried the bowl of my tears

I have to be grateful for the friend who could sit through it all

Through the blazing sun where we let nature take its course

Where we sit until such corruption that we need a pall

Being saved from this mortal life that takes beauty so quick
and easily

That in our foolish Time of youth we may finally see it
vicariously

-to my best friend

Rebone

V. ALONE BUT NOT LONELY

Try not to avoid your feelings, try to face the troubles that keep staring at you, making you uncomfortable. Face them, face your thoughts, face your sadness, your happiness, depression, the insomnia that takes your sleep.

It is after all, a rite of passage.

Allow yourself to heal.

-things we go through before we die

INTERNAL BLEEDING

It takes all the freedom; I cannot be me.

It is a trouble I cannot fathom,

Salt water has washed away everything away, it's in the sea.

I cannot even see my face anymore; it is stained by my sins.

Like the sunflower I am bent by the light,

Struggling to accept the good that comes to me.

Yet I get lost, and I am attracted to the darkness that
enhances my pain.

I am bleeding just so I could feel.

I am breathing because I have hope to heal.

Maybe we are all in the gutter

Yet I see those who smile more than me,

Their smiles kill me, as I sit here reminiscing.

Hoping to find the reason to smile as well.

ROLLING STONE

I'm tired of being the giver

I'm tired of acting like all of the shit I condone is glitter

I'm tired of lying to myself that everything will be better

When after all this time I feel the same

And when I am left in that darkness bitter,

I am the only one left to blame.

All of the things I thought I stood for

All of the company I thought had my back,

Proved me wrong and became the worst enemies,

They became the gas that suffocated me, yet it was the one I
needed to breath.

So tell me if I'm wrong,

Tell me if loving myself should have been more than a choice.

Tell me if loving myself could have been my one true shot at
happiness.

Because I chased lilacs and coconuts,

But in the end, I got thorns and a broken heart.

I'm sorry if I offended you,

I'm sorry if finally sitting at my throne is bothering you

But I have a crown to wear and the world to conquer

To conquer my world and all the golden parts of myself I have
been longing to see

I'm trying my best to mend a soul that has been shattering

I'm trying to tell myself all the 'I love you"s that have been
pending

Only this time I'll be taking time, to find myself

I'll be taking time to love myself.

Because I am tired of being a broken bone,

I am tired of being your rolling stone.

In the greyness of the blue

On that day, on that sombre rainy day,

I see myself in that case, with no more strength to pray.

With no more than a despondent family,

Their tears drop for my long-lasted life vicariously.

On that day, wear my favourite colours.

Alas! It will be the greatest of honours.

Do not cry for me, be joyful for my once felt presence,

Say my name with ecstatic extravagance.

On that day, when I meet my fatal flaws,

Beneath the dreaded dry dirt are the deepest cores.

Of wet soil and deepening darkness,

At the white gate of absolute starkness.

Be it the biggest small of celebration,

Lay me down and let go with true elation.

Dine thus in thee end, the simplest meal,

Take care of the treasure that Time could steal.

WALLFLOWER

Always falling to their knees,

Leaving yourself behind.

The blow of hell's kiss.

A whole you cannot bind.

Your sword is not shining anymore,

It is stained by your blood.

And all that burns to the core,

A pain that haunts you in the dark.

But for your love you will be remembered,

For your smile you shall be embraced.

Your life without question, all that you surrendered.

A happy sadness, all that will be engraved.

And through all of it you will rise at any hour,

All the perks of being a wallflower.

The stars are out of place

I wrote a letter to the other side.

Telling them of all the things I see

All of the things that enhance the pain

All of the things that make my wounds more alive.

The stars are out of place

My world has run out of grace,

I am only moving at your pace,

But I am not your special case.

I wished that you had been the one

To discover the true mystery of my life.

The one who understood why I used to sit alone

The one who understood why I have been fighting all along.

But you also never trusted me with the real you

I was busy selling the only sun I will ever have

Letting it get swallowed, it was not a pleasant view.

The bittersweet memories,

It was the marvel and beauty of love.

The astronomy of our expanding universe.

Now I am left to pick up the pieces above.

Rich Spirit

The soul wishes, the soul desires

It wishes to be clean to be whole.

But there are things that chip away

That change its beauty with wildfires

They give irresistible pleasure, an irresistible thing

The often-forgotten truth about life is the purest soul does not exist.

Because this filthy world cannot be the metric to measure such a delicate thing.

We stand here on our own, limping and limping

With no guidance whatsoever of how to lead this life

Yet we are reminded of the sins, all our inequities

The irony, is that sins are the ones that make us happy

So then tell me what life is, if you should sacrifice yourself

We tend to hide our deepest affections

Because in another place of the ending of us

Our desires have the most hurtful rejections.

The land of the undying

I yearn for things so far away from me.

I dream of a place I have been but once before.

I want the best for my soul, body and mind,

I want the best for myself.

But I cannot get that if I am dying inside,

I am on an unscrewed impetus,

I am screwed and I am screaming inside!

I am screaming for freedom, peace!

And I am screaming even more,

For I want to be in the land of the undying.

A haven I created on loneliest days,

When nothing or anyone can take me back to my normal state.

I can live, I can sing, dance, smile, blush and flourish.

I have no flaws.

I am perfect because I am alone.

I do not have to compare or be compared.

These impediments are no less than the salt that lies between
my tear bags and my eyes,

But I still wipe myself and come back a better man.

And I say unto you, visit the land,

It may not be the land of the undying.

But be certain you are alone,

Because true happiness comes when you find it from within.

Painless

I walk the streets all day, no wonder

The images running inside my hide make me suffer

I pay no attention, I've no mind to make a martyr

With infinite pity in my eyes that I'm not to barter

I stay inside, listening to the silence of that harmony

I have been here before is the irony

Hoping to escape the dauntless agony

"it feels good for a while" so the say

I cannot be free forever, the dream is only a trap

My tongue will forever know its sweet taste

And attractive road without a map

Let all my senses not go to waste

Between Love and loss

I have walked through the sombre storm

Breathed in destiny through the dull air

For it was heaven that came to deform

And took my Time and Love so fair

Death sits in between the rotten

And the love that comes at her entry

In her eyes there are things forgotten

She implores heaven to give amnesty

Yet love is a Timeless vital force

That demands to be felt in all depth

They say mourning is a hopeless cause

And all salty tears demand to be wept

I may walk through the winds of sorrow

But Love gives me strength for tomorrow

Thoughts of Love

My mind is lost in Spring

Blooming dreamily to the thought of you

My heart; the leaves of an autumn tree

That fall vigorously under the blue

If my mind is of Spring's delight

It shall never know nightmares in my days

If my heart knows the leaves of autumn

It shall always fall in your praise

Alone, but not lonely

I want to be on my own

I want to really taste freedom

I want to you to shut the door

I want you to leave me be

I am not pushing you away

I only want to be alone

I want to be in touch in myself

I want to taste salt water from my eyes

I want the water to wash away

To remove the second face I put on to make you smile

I want to feel it all, all of me!!!!!
I want to feel my depression, my insecurities, my broken
heart from that one relationship I told myself I had healed
from.

I want to feel everything I've been avoiding during the day

I want the darkness in this room to mask the memory that
this moment ever even happened

I want to be alone, alone with my emotions.

Untitled

I have reached the limit of my art

Wherein the search for love has failed

In this time I dare not abuse mine heart

It has suffered enough like a bird that's caged

I remember the trying times in the pursuit

That have always bore a promise of their own

All my lovers were there for my suit

But none of them were worthy of my throne

My beloved, I have reached the limit of my art

Thou have shown passion through all the years

But not fervent enough, in the end we part

My soul is left shattered and drowning in tears

VI. WHEN WE ARE FINALLY THERE

Sometimes in our lives we will realise that we are worth so much more, and we deserve the best that life could offer. We shall understand that life was always meant to be soft, love was meant to be real, and happiness was meant to be true and

pure.

-     growth is inevitable, but you can also
      choose how you want to grow

La vi en rose

In the excess of that house

And the murk of that morning divine,

I stand in all Holiness to hear my vows

The staining words I am soon to define.

In the pink and in golden robes

I dare to leave my current grade,

That in all things I had foolish hopes

My new telescopic eyes would invade.

I duel with the air and waters

My prophetic and profound summons,

My journey as I look to the altars

The fiery and demanding colours,

Now here I am in that Holiness

Living with clean spirit and sound mind,

Do not confuse my silence with loneliness

For with the heavens my soul shall bind

Light

Happier Times that give life

So mother nature gave us might

That in the suspending wonder of our strife

She blessed our hearts with eternal light

Our eyes glimmer in excitement

What is before our eyes is nothing of morn'

Our besotted hearts quiver in surprise

For even the moon stayed till dawn

Light that gives us the innocence we seek

The birds singing to comfort us in our strife

We are giving our eyes, stunned as we cannot speak

It helps us forget the things we do not like

Eternal light gives us eternal might

The strength to soldier on

The courage to stand at the top

With the picture of us shining ever so bright

Belted

Enhance my pain my shadowing light

Praise bounteous if it be of Holy might

Then I would retreat to gain my strength

Being it from the source of tremendous stealth

On a Sunday it was, how awkward the day

I was from the temple of unnumbered promises

We sang songs in praise - fell down on our knees to pray

We put our hearts at the altar - the greatest of premises

And I walked home with clean and rich spirit

Upon my arrival I discovered the news that destroyed my heart

Oh death! If I too should go then so be it

For in no way I thought that she and I would part

You did not break; you left my heart melted

You left me, broken, bare and belted

Mother

My one true miracle in this void

That God took so quickly from me

I have been a slave to pain

I forgot I am my own master

My one true miracle in this void

That God took so quickly from me

Should I fight what am I to gain?

Would this hole be filled any faster?

My one true miracle in this void

That God took so quickly from me

If He had the strength to break this chain

Then I beg Him in peace to return my Mother

WHEN WE ARE FINALLY THERE

There comes a time in life when you look back

When you remember everything that has happened

When you cave in to all the bad things and the good things that passed.

All your flaws and perfects.

And maybe wonder if what you are feeling right now will last

Does this life ever get enough?

You do not know

Does sadness ever come to a halt?

You do not know

But just maybe what you ought to know is that

There is a little infinity for all-

There is **indeed** happiness, joy, love, peace and prosperity.

Do not give up just yet, do not be afraid!

Embrace the uncertainty, thrive for greatness.

Ignore the noise and simply move with ease.

VII. UNCHARTERED

Find peace in the craziness you find in your thoughts; these things make the beautiful parts of you.

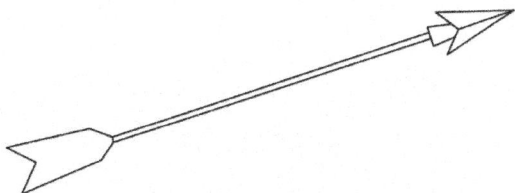

-the eternal verities of my heart

A song of Dragons

All dragons roar as one

And in flight are the greatest of birds

No! they are not birds under the sun

They are reptiles of exciting projectile and returns

They are the free that live as they should

But man encapsulates them to try to put their fire away

Only their godflame burns fortresses like wood

In the end the enemy has a price to pay

They are the marvellous beast

That take the air and gladly beyond

Their fight in celebration of a perfect feast

Still in search of a fiery Lord

Let you down

There is a company in me I hate

Of distant voices that grow closer

Being so close to me as I ascend my stage

I am sorry you deemed me a loser

I'm sorry that I let you down

The disappoint was not really my own doing

But sadly I could not wear your crown

I am still afraid, if you care for my healing

I am scared of the things seen by my blind eyes

I am scared of the things heard by my deaf ears

They are mad things to you, but art to me

Because the pain lets me find beauty in me

What is inside of me is true art

It is not abstract asI feel every sensation

You will never understand why I let you down

In the end, that is why we part.

Concert of broken strings

In the hopes to find a silver lining

There erupts chaos in that cacophony

Emotions spinning and breaking octaves

Primal and naked like creatures in caves

When she played the strings she healed my wounds

In the climax of the melody, she blew the winds

The beautiful pieces of her heart kept me

Sane in that madness when I had lost my key

When our love subsided and the song calmed

It was never that our loved was ended

Even with her broken heart I stayed loved

In her land of unforgiving song is where I landed

Frozen Lips

You came into my life so instantaneously

The first time I saw you was in the most awkward of moments

I still remember you were looking for something and I was
bound to assist

And seeing your innocent and irresistible face I did help

On the sunny side, fire ran through my veins

You set my heart on the peak of the mountain

It was a feeling I had ignored for so long in my life,

because I knew where it led

But something with you was different, I couldn't let go of this
feeling

I was incredibly enthralled

Yet when I saw you the next day you revealed your true self,
you were different

You were still the person of yesterday but something in the
way you talked had suddenly shifted

I did not know whether to like this part of you or loathe it

But I found little comfort, that I was not to feel infinite pity of
the innocent you anymore

I don't know

I think I love you

But I don't like

How you leave me bare

Cold and with frozen lips

Some days to go by

Some days to go by without the taste of your honey

Without the smile that looks at me like the sunflower looks at the sun

Blushing fervently and bending towards a more strong power

Some days to go by without the grapes that turn to wine which so makes me drunk in love

Without the trees that bore the fruits that taste of the passion between us my love

Some days, some painful days to go by... without you

Uncharted

You make me the imperfect pieces of my heart

You are the puzzle and the one that solves

You know rightfully how to play your part

You are the one where my mind revolves

My fair maid, so far can we escape

Beyond the boundaries of this chartered earth

Let us! take the journey of such bitter taste

That tomorrow and together, we may face death

Oh! My dying life, which so in the forest spawns

That land and the ugliness of that filthy river

Where they do not sit, the hopeless and dying herons

This filigree of death, where even the lifeless quiver

This image, this fine line; not all is grotesque

So patience dear love, you dare not to protest

Finite

Nothing ever lasts forever

Like the water in the ocean

Even one's greatest treasure

Fades away in the open

About the author

Ikageng Pheko is a passionate young man who grew up in Thaba Nchu, in the Free State. As a young and maturing boy he wanted his voice to be heard as he believed he has a lot to offer this world.

After losing his parents and his beloved sister, he started writing as a way to express his feelings. He attempted to write a novel but could never finish because of his undying commitment to his education. He then turned to poetry, which he so believes that his emotions cannot only be expressed but his work would be easily relatable to others.

This book reflects on some of the sad and happy moments in his life. His poesy is seen as a 'breakthrough' through mental and emotional struggle. A promise that there is indeed hope for the greener future. There lies a little hope in every man that can be seen in the midst of our pain.

To my best friends

-thank you

.

Made in the USA
Las Vegas, NV
22 March 2023